Would You Rather?

WILD

EDITION

Try Not To Laugh Challenge
BONUS PLAY

Join our Joke Club and get the Bonus Play PDF!

Simply send us an email to:

TNTLPublishing@gmail.com

and you will get the following:

- 10 Hilarious Would You Rather Questions
- An entry in our Monthly Giveaway of a $50 Amazon Gift card!

We draw a new winner each month and will contact you via email!

Good luck!

Welcome to
The Try Not to Laugh Challenge Would You Rather?
WILD EDITION

RULES:

• Face your opponent and decide who is 'Player 1' and 'Player 2'.

• Starting with 'Player 1', read the Would You Rather question aloud and pick an answer. The same player will then explain why they chose that answer in the most hilarious or wacky way possible!

• If the reason makes 'Player 2' laugh, then a laugh point is scored!

• Take turns going back and forth, then mark your total laugh points at the end of each round!

• Whoever gets the most laugh points is officially crowned the 'Laugh Master'!

• If ending with a tie, finish with the Tie-Breaker round for WINNER TAKES ALL!

Most importantly, have fun and be SILLY!

REMEMBER, these scenarios listed in the book are solely for fun and games! Please do <u>NOT</u> attempt any of the crazy scenarios in this book.

ROUND

1

Player ❶

Would you rather be able to turn invisible only when your eyes are closed, OR be able to breathe underwater only when you stick out your tongue?

Laugh Point_____ /1

Would you rather swim in the belly of a giant whale OR have a mini whale swim in your belly?

Laugh Point_____ /1

Player 1

(DON'T FORGET TO EXPLAIN YOUR ANSWERS!)

Would you rather be able to start a fire with your mind OR make water appear with your hands?

Laugh Point____/1

Would you rather have six fingers OR three eyes?

Laugh Point____/1

Pass the book to Player 2! →

Player ❷

Would you rather live in a mansion made of 100 tiny rooms, OR just one giant room?

Laugh Point____ /1

Would you rather win a million dollars, but have to give it all away OR win a luxury vacation, but have to go with someone you despise?

Laugh Point____ /1

Player 2

(DON'T FORGET TO EXPLAIN YOUR ANSWERS!)

Would you rather learn that your neighbor is an alien OR that your best friend sleeps in a nest, in a tree?

Laugh Point_____ /1

Would you rather be the parent to a hundred children, OR be the King with no heir?

Laugh Point_____ /1

Player **1** _____ **/4**
ROUND TOTAL

Player **2** _____ **/4**
ROUND TOTAL

_____
ROUND CHAMPION

ROUND
2

Player 1

Would you rather not speak for a year OR shout every time you spoke for a year?

Laugh Point____/1

Would you rather wrestle with an alligator for 3 minutes OR have a 10-minute boxing match with a kangaroo?

Laugh Point____/1

Player 1

Would you rather have your face on the dollar bill, OR have a state named after you?

Laugh Point____ /1

Would you rather be able to reflect the sun with shiny skin, OR glow in the dark?

Laugh Point____ /1

Pass the book to Player 2! →

Player 2

Would you rather see 3 days into the future, OR travel 3 days into the past?

Laugh Point____/1

Would you rather shrink down to any size, OR have the ability to leap over mountains?

Laugh Point____/1

Player 2

Would you rather live on the moon by yourself, OR on an island inside a giant volcano with a community?

Laugh Point____ /1

Would you rather only listen to your favorite song for the rest of your life OR be able to listen to 10 new songs every week, but your parents pick them?

Laugh Point____ /1

Player ⭐**1**⭐ _____ **/4**
ROUND TOTAL

Player ⭐**2**⭐ _____ **/4**
ROUND TOTAL

_____
ROUND
CHAMPION

ROUND

3

Player 1

Would you rather cartwheel across a tightrope, OR backflip across a freeway?

Laugh Point_____/1

Would you rather bump into Sasquatch in the woods, OR discover the Loch Ness monster lives in the lake where you're swimming?

Laugh Point_____/1

Player 1

(DON'T FORGET TO EXPLAIN YOUR ANSWERS!)

Would you rather have a bird pop out of your mouth every hour, on the hour (like a human cuckoo clock), OR have to clean your house by sucking up dirt with your mouth (like a human vacuum) for a week?

Laugh Point____ /1

Would you rather go hiking on a live volcano OR be stuck outside during a tornado?

Laugh Point____ /1

Pass the book to Player 2! →

Player ②

(DON'T FORGET TO EXPLAIN YOUR ANSWERS!)

Would you rather cross a shark tank while blindfolded on a tightrope, OR dangle upside down from a helicopter over the ocean?

Laugh Point____ /1

Would you rather create a new color, OR create a new taste?

Laugh Point____ /1

Player ❷

Would you rather discover a Bigfoot footprint at your nearest park OR a Bigfoot handprint on your back door?

Laugh Point____ /1

Would you rather live in a giant, edible peach OR a giant clam shell with pearls?

Laugh Point____ /1

Player ★①★ _____ /4
ROUND TOTAL

Player ★②★ _____ /4
ROUND TOTAL

_____
ROUND
CHAMPION

ROUND

4

Player 1

Would you rather have a ceiling fan that can turn into a helicopter, OR have a washing machine that can turn into a submarine?

Laugh Point_____/1

Would you rather live forever as a grasshopper, OR live 9 lives as an unlucky cat?

Laugh Point_____/1

Player ❶

Would you rather play basketball with a group of 9-foot tall giants, OR play baseball without a bat?

Laugh Point_____/1

Would you rather be stuck in an elevator with someone who has really bad gas for 6 hours, OR trapped on the roof of a skyscraper overnight?

Laugh Point_____/1

Pass the book to Player 2! →

Player ❷

Would you rather be able to breathe underwater OR breathe in outer space?

Laugh Point____ /1

Would you rather have a mouth that transmits radio, OR eyes that projected movies?

Laugh Point____ /1

Player ❷

Would you rather stay in your hometown for the rest of your life OR visit every country in the world, but never be able to visit home?

Laugh Point_____/1

Would you rather wake up one morning with tiny wings OR huge antlers?

Laugh Point_____/1

31

Player **1** /4
ROUND TOTAL

Player **2** /4
ROUND TOTAL

ROUND CHAMPION

ROUND
5

Player ①

(DON'T FORGET TO EXPLAIN YOUR ANSWERS!)

Would you rather ice skate blindfolded OR wrestle with your hands tied behind your back?

Laugh Point_____ /1

Would you rather sleepwalk through a cave of 1,000 bats OR through a den of 3 hungry wolves?

Laugh Point_____ /1

Player ❶

Would you rather have hair made out of dry spaghetti OR arms made out of chopped wood?

Laugh Point_____ /1

Would you rather have a mustache made out of living caterpillars, OR a hat made out of 3 living snakes?

Laugh Point_____ /1

Pass the book to Player 2! →

Player 2

Would you rather jump off of a 50-foot cliff into the ocean, OR bungee jump from the world's highest bridge?

Laugh Point____/1

Would you rather wear underwear made out of bologna OR underwear made from tumbleweeds?

Laugh Point____/1

Player 2

Would you rather have x-ray vision OR perfect night vision?

Laugh Point_____ /1

Would you rather be able to teleport to any planet in the universe, OR shrink to the size of atoms?

Laugh Point_____ /1

Player ★★①★★   /4
_____
ROUND TOTAL

Player ★★②★★   /4
_____
ROUND TOTAL

_____
ROUND
CHAMPION

ROUND

6

Player ❶

Would you rather snowboard down a mountain during an active avalanche, OR go kayaking down Niagara Falls?

Laugh Point_____ /1

Would you rather become an alien yourself OR have an alien for a best friend?

Laugh Point_____ /1

Player 1

(DON'T FORGET TO EXPLAIN YOUR ANSWERS!)

Would you rather breathe fire out of your nostrils OR shoot lasers from your eyes?

Laugh Point____ /1

Would you rather go sledding down a hill of lava OR waterski in alligator-infested waters?

Laugh Point____ /1

Pass the book to Player 2! →

Player ②

Would you rather have an extra toe on each foot OR an extra thumb on each hand?

Laugh Point_____/1

Would you rather have to say everything you think out loud OR have to hear everyone else's thoughts constantly?

Laugh Point_____/1

Player ②

Would you rather have to sing everything you say OR only be able to communicate through interpretive dance?

Laugh Point____ /1

Would you rather bounce from place to place on streets made of trampolines OR be able to travel anywhere by zip line?

Laugh Point____ /1

Player **1** _____ /4
ROUND TOTAL

Player **2** _____ /4
ROUND TOTAL

_____
ROUND
CHAMPION

ROUND

7

Player 1

Would you rather sleep in a cave with 100 snakes OR sleep on a mountain with a family of bears?

Laugh Point_____/1

Would you rather be able to teleport, but land in sewage every time you do OR be able to fly, but be covered in bird poop during your flight?

Laugh Point_____/1

Player 1

Would you rather everyone in the world speak exactly the same OR think exactly the same?

Laugh Point_____ /1

Would you rather live where endless amounts of dog hair fall from the sky OR live where all grass is made of shredded cell phones?

Laugh Point_____ /1

Pass the book to Player 2! →

Player ②

Would you rather leave footprints everywhere you have walked, OR leave handprints on everything you have touched?

Laugh Point_____ /1

Would you rather be lost in space, OR lost at sea?

Laugh Point_____ /1

48

Player 2

Would you rather be able to play every instrument that exists, OR be able to speak every language in the world?

Laugh Point____ /1

Would you rather live where every walkway was made of broken LEGO's, OR live where every house in town was a jack-in-the-box that unexpectedly goes off?

Laugh Point____ /1

Player ⭐**1**⭐ _____ **/4**
ROUND TOTAL

Player ⭐**2**⭐ _____ **/4**
ROUND TOTAL

_____
ROUND
CHAMPION

ROUND

8

Player 1

Would you rather dangle from the minute hand of London's Big Ben Clock Tower, while it slowly counts down, OR hang from the edge of the Grand Canyon, as it is being swallowed by a sinkhole?

Laugh Point_____ /1

Would you rather be able to read your pet's mind OR your parents' mind?

Laugh Point_____ /1

Player 1

Would you rather light all the stars in the sky by hand, forever OR paint every cloud in the sky 24 hours a day, for the rest of your life?

Laugh Point_____ /1

Would you rather be trapped in the body of an underwater statue OR doomed to sail the tides, forever trapped inside a sinking piano?

Laugh Point_____ /1

Pass the book to Player 2! →

Player ②

Would you rather count grains of rice in a barrel, OR hand paint the entire length of the Grand Canyon?

Laugh Point_____/1

Would you rather be trapped inside the mind of a baby doll for the rest of your life OR be stuck inside a toy race car, that happens to be the dog's favorite chew toy?

Laugh Point_____/1

Player ②

Would you rather be able to tell the future, but have no one believe you OR have everyone convinced you're telling the future, but really you're just making it up?

Laugh Point_____ /1

Would you rather be born with a built-in flashlight in the middle of your forehead (that never turns off) OR have a built-in button on your butt, that screams like a hyena whenever you sit down?

Laugh Point_____ /1

Player **1** _____ /4
ROUND TOTAL

Player **2** _____ /4
ROUND TOTAL

_____ ROUND CHAMPION

ROUND
9

Player 1

Would you rather drop your phone into a landfill, filled with exact clones of your device OR lose your game system in a pile of nonfunctional replicas and have to test out ALL of them to find yours?

Laugh Point____ /1

Would you rather be able to change into any animal OR change into any other human?

Laugh Point____ /1

Player 1

Would you rather live in a big house that floats in the air and ride on the back of a giant eagle to get around, OR live in an underwater castle and ride on a dolphin?

Laugh Point_____ /1

Would you rather be King/Queen of the planet Mars, but be thirsty all the time OR be told what to do on Earth, but have lots of tasty drinks?

Laugh Point_____ /1

Pass the book to Player 2! →

Player ❷

Would you rather your parents picked your name by using the full quote from a fortune cookie OR after the first thing they saw when you were born?

Laugh Point____/1

Would you rather ride in a topless Safari car with raw meat in your pocket, while visiting the lion den OR hang from a bottomless elevator, that's quickly being dropped into a cobra pit?

Laugh Point____/1

Player 2

(DON'T FORGET TO EXPLAIN YOUR ANSWERS!)

Would you rather your shadow be evil and the only way to stay safe is to stay away from all light, OR your shadow burn everything you pass, leaving evidence of your presence everywhere?

Laugh Point____ /1

Would you rather look into any mirror and see one thing from your future OR look at a photograph and relive that moment in real time?

Laugh Point____ /1

Player ★**①**★ /4
ROUND TOTAL

Player ★**②**★ /4
ROUND TOTAL

ROUND
CHAMPION

ROUND

10

Player 1

Would you rather be locked inside a small bird cage with 50 buzzards, OR be trapped inside a greenhouse where every inch is covered in poison ivy?

Laugh Point____ /1

Would you rather surf on an ocean made of jelly OR ski down a mountain of spaghetti and meatballs?

Laugh Point____ /1

Player ①

Would you rather your job be to heat every volcano, one pot of lava at a time OR have to refill the ocean with one saltbox at a time?

Laugh Point___ /1

Would you rather fight 1 giant praying mantis OR an army of skeletons?

Laugh Point___ /1

Pass the book to Player 2! →

Player 2

Would you rather your hair be made of dandelion puffs and some of it blows away every time the wind blows, OR your skin be made of tissue paper and every small movement rips a piece off?

Laugh Point_____/1

Would you rather ski down a 500-foot slope OR go down a 500-foot waterslide?

Laugh Point_____/1

Player ❷

Would you rather there be as many different, unpredictable copies of you as there are pieces of confetti during New Years, OR have 2 clones that act like you, but always make you look bad?

Laugh Point____ /1

Would you rather stand in a snake den for 1 minute OR stand on a fire ant colony while barefoot for 10 seconds?

Laugh Point____ /1

Player ★①★ _____ **/4**
ROUND TOTAL

Player ★②★ _____ **/4**
ROUND TOTAL

_____
ROUND
CHAMPION

Add up all your points from each round.
The PLAYER with the most points is crowned
The Laugh Master!

In the event of a tie, continue to the Round 11
for the tie-breaker round!

Player **1** _____
GRAND TOTAL

Player **2** _____
GRAND TOTAL

_____

The
Laugh Master

ROUND

11

TIE-BREAKER

(WINNER TAKES ALL!)

Player ❶

Would you rather go to a zombie circus where the acts attack the audience, OR go to a magic show where the magician turns the audience into hungry ghouls?

Laugh Point_____ /1

Would you rather every crayon in the world melt and everyone has to swim through a sea of wax, OR every piece of chalk in the world smashes causing a constant dust storm?

Laugh Point_____ /1

Player 1

Would you rather wrap yourself in sandwich meat and let a flock of hungry seagulls eat it off of you OR cover yourself in chunky strawberry syrup and let the insects feast?

Laugh Point____/1

Would you rather wake up with a snake in your bed OR fall asleep knowing there's a tarantula somewhere in your room?

Laugh Point____/1

Pass the book to Player 2! →

Player 2

Would you rather have Ms. Frizzle from The Magic School Bus as your teacher OR Mrs. Puff from Spongebob Squarepants?

Laugh Point_____/1

Would you rather be able to grow cotton candy OR candy corn in your garden?

Laugh Point_____/1

Player 2

Would you rather stand outside in the heavy rain for 10 minutes OR stand outside during a hailstorm for 1 minute?

Laugh Point____ /1

Would you rather be able to turn your head all the way around like an owl, OR be able to move your eyes one at a time like a chameleon?

Laugh Point____ /1

Add up all your points from Round 11.
The PLAYER with the most points is crowned
The Laugh Master!

Player ①   /4
_____
ROUND TOTAL

Player ②   /4
_____
ROUND TOTAL

_____
The
Laugh Master

Check out our other joke books!

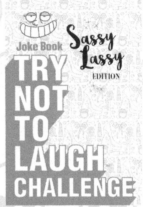

Visit on Amazon Store at:
www.Amazon.com/author/CrazyCorey

Made in the USA
Coppell, TX
13 December 2019

12887525R00046